Aging Into Bliss

Discovering the Wisdom and Joy of Your Timeless Nature

Aging into Bliss

Discovering the Wisdom and Joy of Your Timeless Nature

Christopher Foster

www.thehappyseeker.com

Published by Singing Spirit Books, Centennial, Colorado 80122 USA

First published 2012
ISBN – 13:978-0-9711796-1-5

Book design and layout by:
KeyBoard Graphic Design, Print and Web
www.maddi.ca

Foreword by Carol Leavenworth,
Jungian psychotherapist

Also by Christopher Foster:

The Raven Who Spoke with God

Winds Across the Sky

Bearers of the Sun

One Heart, One Way (A biography)

A Time for Heroes (Poems)

The Transcendent Nation (Poems)

To JoAnn and Durwin

Special thanks to Elizabeth Nunn, Carol Leavenworth and Maddi Newman

Author's note

I want to thank all those who have helped make this book possible and say how much I have enjoyed hearing from many people who are discovering, like me, that aging can be a door to remarkable happiness and fulfillment.

Johanna Fourie, a white South African now living in China, sums up this central premise of my book beautifully in the following comment:

"I am 69 now and it's true. As the years go by, we discover day by day our true and real colors! Every day I find myself less impressed by this busy worldly rush – even as I become more interested in discovering real values, real people, and real happenings.

"Trifling affairs just don't make it into my life anymore, while close family, friends and happy moments increase in value. And of course Nature and the Creator of all things in heaven and on earth are becoming increasingly an intimate part of my life. I really find aging a wonderful season to be living in!"

CONTENTS

Foreword

By Carol Leavenworth, Jungian psychotherapist

In his final years of driving, my father Frank would climb into his big white Buick for a trip into town, insert the key into the ignition and pause before backing out of the garage.

"Where am I?" he would muse.

Then, "Where am I going?"

And finally he would ask himself, "How do I get there?"

Dad wasn't one to give advice or pass along life lessons. But here, I thought, was some important wisdom. These are questions we could all be asking ourselves and not just when we're in the car.

I learned a lot from Dad down the years. He taught me highway driving and how to balance a checkbook along with many other things. But his most important lessons – like this one – were imparted indirectly.

Sometimes toward the end of his days, I would ask him to tell me about the essential things that his long life taught him. He would become shy and change the subject.

Maybe he was afraid that if he opened up, he would be misunderstood or dismissed. Probably this had happened to him before. If it had, he would not have been alone.

Young and old, we are all victims of a pervasive and insidious cultural ageism. Our elders are trivialized and often ignored. We look at the elderly and see bodies that are in decline. We see white hair and wrinkled skin. And we want to turn away.

We tend to think of the old as failing adults with nothing much to say that is relevant to busy adult lives. We haven't been taught that there is another stage of psychological development waiting for us all beyond adulthood. We seldom hear about the happiness that characterizes this final period of life. We don't understand that our elders know the answers to questions we have been asking ourselves since adolescence.

This is why I was excited when Christopher Foster offered to share his latest work, *Aging into Bliss – Discovering the Wisdom* and *Joy of Your Timeless Nature.* Chris is in the vanguard of a growing number of elders committed to letting the rest of us in on important realizations to be found on the other side of the great demarcation between adulthood and elderhood.

Aging into Bliss goes to the heart of the mystery surrounding life's final developmental stage. In his first chapter, Chris reveals key secrets to the joy and peace of mind that led him to the bliss he is discovering in his later years.

Chris goes on to tell us exactly what his personal experience has taught him about the love within each one of us and the happiness that is hiding everywhere in plain sight. And he doesn't stop there. He shares specific details about his personal path to profound inner wisdom – the wisdom he believes any of us may discover deep within.

Acknowledging that each individual's journey is unique, Chris encourages us to seek out our own happiness and bliss. With the confidence that arises out of authentic personal experience, he points the way to self-realization. And he shows us exactly how to explore this path for ourselves.

When I asked my ninety-year-old father to tell me his secret to long life, he answered, "Don't die."

I would add this to Dad's advice: "Don't die before you read Chris Foster's amazing little book *Aging into Bliss.*"

Carol Leavenworth is a psychotherapist in Denver, Colorado. For helpful resources and articles on aging visit her website at: www.desperatecaregivers.com

CHAPTER 1

The Secret Bliss of Aging

> *"Follow your bliss and the universe will open doors where there were only walls."*
> – Joseph Campbell

I have learned many lessons in my life. But the most remarkable lesson of all is learning that aging, despite its challenges, can be a door to increasing happiness and fulfillment.

As I enter my 80's I experience a "secret bliss" based not so much in outer circumstances but in a growing awareness of the timeless wisdom and joy of my true nature.

I call it "secret" simply because it is something that doesn't seem to be talked about much in our society. Aging gets a bad rap, for the most part. As Linda Fried of the International Longevity Center at Columbia University said recently, "We have such a human aversion to getting old; it's associated with death, and death is scary. But as a society, we have not had the conversations we need to have. There are huge opportunities there."

It’s my hope that this book, based in insights and experiences from my blog with new material added, will contribute to the conversation that as Dr. Fried says, is so urgently needed right now. It’s a conversation about aging, yes, but also about who we truly are – and what our purpose is on this beautiful, troubled planet.

My life has not been easy. I’ve had my share of tribulation. But I’ve learned that wisdom is within each one of us, and that as we listen to its quiet voice in our heart, a way through fear and doubt will emerge.

I’ve learned, too, that a new kind of courage is required in these days. It’s the courage to change our mind and allow new ideas and possibilities to open up in us even if they conflict with commonly-held views or attitudes.

Steven E. Mock, of the Department of Health Studies and Gerontology at the University of Waterloo in Ontario, revealed in a 2011 study that our attitudes toward aging directly influence our psychological well-being. He pointed out how contemporary North American culture has a "largely unflattering impression" of the aging process, and these negative stereotypes affect some middle-aged and older adults' attitudes toward aging.

Regardless of our age, we have an opportunity to reverse these negative stereotypes in our lives – just as many, many people are already doing in inspiring and remarkable ways all across the face of this planet.

In my experience I have difficult days, of course. Painful feelings still arise. Challenges still arise. Aging takes its toll in various ways.

But always present, sometimes in the background and sometimes in the foreground, is a growing awareness, as I say, of the underlying wisdom and joy of my true nature. It is something that never changes. It is always here. Disturbances of various kinds erupt from time to time but this reality is undisturbed by any of it.

It is the bliss of our timeless presence and it is the birthright of each one of us.

I can honestly say I am happier now than I have ever been in my life. As Denver psychotherapist, Carol Leavenworth, writes in her Foreword to this book, it is time to stop seeing the elderly as failed or failing adults and recognize that as the population of aging people expands many are experiencing a significant level of joy and well-being. They are moving, as Carol says, beyond "adulthood" into a more advanced state some call "gerotranscendence."

As I mentioned earlier, I've had my share of trauma and loss. I didn't think I would survive when my late wife, Joy, suffered a fatal stroke as we were flying home to British Columbia after celebrating our 25th wedding anniversary in the Caribbean.

Nor did I think I would survive when the spiritual community in British Columbia that had been my home for 36 years collapsed after the death of its leader. At the age of 63 – with virtually no material resources – I had no choice but to return to the outside world I abandoned in the idealism of youth.

Then, in 2005, just when I thought my life was back to normal – I was living happily in Colorado with my new wife, JoAnn – the first of two terrible year-long periods of depression struck suddenly one evening out of the blue.

I was watching the evening news and all was well when without warning I suffered a severe two-hour anxiety attack. I retired to my bed, where I lay for two hours in JoAnn's arms shivering with heat, cold, and terrifying memories of the Blitz before I was evacuated from London in WWII.

I am 6-foot tall, but in the days that followed I watched helpless as my weight plummeted from 150 pounds to 128 pounds. No-one seemed able to help me. I thought my life was at an end, and the truth is, I wanted it to end.

And yet I got better from that awful experience somehow, and without medication too. But a couple of years or so later, in 2008, I suffered a repeat occurrence, as bad, and in some ways worse than the first. But once again grace stepped in. As I describe in one of the chapters of this book, there came – in the midst of the anguish and darkness – a moment of beautiful inner stillness that changed my life forever.

Perhaps I was passing through "the dark night of the soul" spoken of through the ages. Perhaps my illness wasn't really a "clinical depression" as diagnosed by the doctors but a spiritual crisis. Frightening though the ordeal was – including a week's stay in a Kaiser mental hospital in Denver – perhaps it was life's way to heal my body and mind from past trauma.

Who knows? I am here now, and I give thanks for all of it. Everything that has happened in my life has helped bring me to this moment where I can share with you the love that is in my heart. It is love for our true nature that calls to each of us in these difficult days regardless of our age.

It is never too soon and never too late to claim your birthright – the birthright of your own blissful, timeless, boundless reality.

CHAPTER 2

The Surprising Potential of Aging

> *"You want me to do something... tell me I can't do it."*
> – Maya Angelou

Does life have to diminish as we grow older? Or can we find ways to keep fit, physically and mentally, and keep growing and expanding our boundaries as we age?

I've been thinking of these things since an unusual encounter at my gym the other day.

I've been doing resistance training for 10 years. It's a lifeline for me. The other day I was finishing up my routine on a machine that targets the abdomen when a young fellow came over to me. He had a friendly smile on his face as he looked at me.

"How old are you?" he asked in a simple, straightforward way. More directly I'm sure than would have happened in the Britain I knew in my youth.

I had never met this man but smiled back and told him my age. He positively beamed and said how happy he was to realize we don't have to go downhill as we age but can stay vigorous and active.

I'm 80, one of many older people who realize they do not have to be subject to stereotypes about aging, and that despite its challenges it can be a time of remarkable promise and opportunity.

I was charmed and delighted last evening when I saw a clip on the evening news of a good-looking 89-year-old man being honored at a graduation ceremony at an American university. How happy and proud he looked, and he deserved to be happy and proud.

Every life is unique. But here are some ways in which I am finding a remarkable potential in aging that I perhaps could not have imagined when I was a young fellow wrapped up in my busy activities and goals:

I am becoming more conscious every day of my true nature. A longing for truth that has been with me since my youth is being fulfilled and I am so grateful.

My appreciation for the magic of little moments is increasing. It takes a very small thing to make me happy – stopping to watch a bird in flight, or chatting for a moment with the serving lady at my coffee shop is more than enough.

My love for people keeps growing. “Everyone’s doing their best,” I say to my wife. Perhaps it’s because I’m not in such a hurry. Perhaps it’s because the passing years and a whole lot of pain have made me more capable of empathy and compassion.

I have always loved Nature, and the lessons she teaches. But I honor her more each day for the gifts she gives so generously. We have a creek just below our townhome complex that flows all year long and I never tire of listening to its sweet sounds as it swirls skillfully past rocks and other obstacles.

I see the past traumas of my life in a new light. I used to think they were terrible and unjust, but now I realize they actually opened a door to greater freedom and happiness.

My love for my wife, JoAnn, deepens and every day I appreciate her strong, caring spirit and wonder how I could be so lucky. Except I don’t think it is luck really. I think a hand of grace brought us together and keeps us together.

And last I see my father in a new light. A beautiful light. I could not connect with him when he lived but I connect with him now and I feel him encouraging me as I live my life. I love him as I love my mother and others who have departed this realm and I know they bless me on my journey.

Our bodies age, yes. But our unconquerable spirit does not age.

CHAPTER 3

Joy's Journey Home

"Death is no more than passing from one room into another. But there's a difference for me, you know. Because in that other room I shall be able to see."
– Helen Keller.

Some people think that death is the end of everything. But I am not one of those people. And the reason – one of the reasons anyway, a very special reason – has to do with Joy, my wife of 25 years, who died suddenly on December 15, 1991.

We were married in a spiritual community in the interior of British Columbia in 1967 and lived there until she died. It was an extraordinary life, a wonderful adventure, sharing with perhaps 100 other kindred spirits in a mutual love of integrity and truth. We had a son, we followed the call of truth, we created a newsletter called Integrity which opened friendships all over the world, and we made nine visits to India.

And then one day – who could have imagined such a thing? – Life plucked Joy from me.

We were flying home to Vancouver, British Columbia, after celebrating our 25th anniversary in the Caribbean. Joy moved to the rear of the plane, saying she had a headache and wanted more room.

Then came the terrifying moment when a stewardess stopped beside me and said my wife didn't look well, and would I please take a look at her. I sat beside Joy but soon realized she was not really present anymore. I tried again and again to reach her, to speak to her, but there was no recognition in her eyes.

She had such a lovely face. Such a lovely smile. But soon I would see them no more. When we reached Vancouver, Joy was rushed to Richmond General Hospital where a doctor, very grave, summoned me to his office. She had suffered a fatal aneurysm and there was nothing they could do to help her. "You must make peace with yourself as best you can," the doctor said.

I was numb from head to toe. I sat with Joy for about four hours before she died but here's the strange thing. Every now and again she would turn her head and look at me. And I swear that more than once she winked at me.

Then came a moment, like sun breaking through a cloud when I sensed she wanted to say something. I bent my head toward her and heard her whisper, soft as a piece of silk falling to the floor, “Home.” It was just one word. But a word I have never forgotten.

I wondered for a moment if she meant she wanted to be taken back to our village in the interior of BC but then I knew it was not that. She was on her way to another realm and wanted me to know all was well.

I have often felt Joy's presence as I continue on with my life and I feel her blessing with me now.

CHAPTER 4

The Buoyant Spirit

> *"The most certain sign of wisdom is cheerfulness."*
> – Michel de Montaigne

The Collins English Dictionary defines *buoyancy* in four ways:

- *The ability to float in a liquid or to rise in a fluid.*
- *(Physics) the property of a fluid to exert an upward force on a body that is wholly or partly submerged in it.*
- *The ability to recover quickly after setback; resilience.*
- *Cheerfulness.*

One of the most dismal days of my life was the day when I was sent to hospital by ambulance for further examination by a local doctor worried how thin and sick I was. I had to go through various tests and then a psychologist came to see me in the emergency ward, and we chatted for a while.

I thought we had quite a good chat, although it troubled me that a uniformed guard with a pistol on his belt was lurking about outside the cubicle where I was lying. What was he doing there? Did he think I might try to damage myself?

In any case after we had chatted for a while the psychologist spoke with my wife, JoAnn, down the hall outside my room.

"She said you were in a clinical depression but she simply couldn't understand why you were so cheerful and had such a buoyant spirit," JoAnn told me later.

I am so thankful for the buoyant spirit that is the birthright of each one of us, part of the Eternal Love that is who we truly are. I love the words of the Spanish nun and mystic, St. Teresa of Avila: "Let nothing disturb thee; Let nothing dismay thee; All things pass; God changeth never."

CHAPTER 5

Changing Our Attitude Toward Fear

> *"Right now, in this moment, just look at yourself briefly with your mind's eye. See if it is not possible, even as you are reading this, to catch just a glimpse out of the corner of your eye of the feeling of you, the you-ness of you, the profound and primal ordinariness of you. See how certain, how literally unquestionable it is that you are here, and how that presence of you here is certain in a way nothing else can ever be.*
>
> *"If you do this once knowingly, you will without fail do it again, and again, and again. And the day will certainly come... when you will notice that the underlying fear of life is dead — an old and false notion about your nature snuffed out by contact with the reality of your nature."*
>
> – John Sherman

Fear has its usefulness, some people say. And perhaps that is true. But there is a paradox in this notion, because fear can also cripple us, and destroy us, or sabotage our lives an inch at a time with its background murmur of worry or discontent, a nagging feeling that something is not quite right with our life.

I have known a lot of anxiety in my life. But the more conscious I become of my true nature the more I realize that our true nature is not fear. Fear dilutes and distracts from our true nature which is love. Love is boundless, timeless and changeless. Love does not die.

There is a law at work here, I find: As love increases, fear decreases.

I am not free of fear. Oh dear no. Anxious feelings still arise. I sometimes think that none of us can be truly free of fear as long as we live in a fearful world.

But as my awareness of my own timeless presence deepens so an underlying sense of calm also deepens and it is one of the most exciting experiences of my life.

I realize that it is possible to change my attitude toward fear, so that when fear arises I see it not as a threat but as a visitor who may have something useful to say, but who above all needs my compassion and love.

I see fear as lost energy that wants to come home. It is frozen energy that wants to be healed and to help us heal too. As Gangaji says in her beautiful book, *The Diamond in Your Pocket*, "When you stop and open to what you have resisted throughout time, you find that fear is not fear. Fear is energy. Fear is space. Fear is the Buddha. It is Christ's heart knocking at your door."

I wish for you what I wish for myself. That together with all kindred spirits everywhere we emerge into an ever deepening experience of the freedom and joy that is our birthright.

There is a longing in so many hearts for stability, and calm, but where is that stability and calm going to come from?

I experience that it comes from within ourselves as we become increasingly conscious of our own reality that, as John Sherman truly says, "is certain in a way nothing else can ever be."

Eternal Love is your birthright. It is our true identity and it calls to each one of us in these troubled times.

CHAPTER 6

How My Big Challenge Boosted My Confidence

> *"Once a month, try something you don't think you'd be good at. You can find such happy surprises."*
> – Dianna Agron

Sometimes, when we take on a new challenge, especially if we are getting into an area where we are not too comfortable in the first place, we really do wonder at times if we will succeed. But how good it feels when we follow that little voice in our heart saying, "You can do it. Trust your own unconquerable spirit, and know that the people you need to help you will appear when you need them."

I bought a new computer recently. I didn't have much choice really. I put it off as long as I could, mind you, because computers are not my strong point. I'm an artistic kind of fellow, I suppose, more at home writing a poem than penetrating the mysteries that make a computer work.

But I'm here to say I'm so happy that computers do work and are part of my world. They make my world so much richer, fuller, and more interesting. Computers didn't exist when my Dad was churning out stories for his newspaper on a battered old typewriter. But now they do exist. And they help me talk to you, and listen to you.

My Dell was 10 years old and like an old dog, a beloved pet, it was getting harder and harder for it just to move at all. It was time for something new. But what to buy? What make, what model? Just trying to decide these questions was challenging enough. But that was just the beginning. There was a new version of Word to understand. A new version of Windows to comprehend. There were new programs to install. There were new versions of old programs to install. Many times I thought I had everything set up properly only to discover there was a whole big piece I hadn't even thought of yet. And so it went. One challenge after another.

But here's what I want to share with you. As I sit here this morning, working on my new computer, I'm filled with so much joy, because this challenge has boosted my confidence. I realize more strongly than ever before that life really does want us to expand our boundaries, regardless of our age. It wants us to keep creating a more fulfilling, happy life for ourselves and our world no matter what.

I'll be honest with you. Using this computer is like driving down the road in a Cadillac (not that I've ever done that, mind you) compared to riding in the back of a battered old pickup.

And so it comes down to this. Life is good. Life is very sweet. Life really does want to bless us, and lead us to a richer, more abundant life. But we have to play our part. We have to keep listening to the wisdom of our own heart. We have to keep going even though part of us might like to quit, or we wonder if we can really do this thing, or if it is really all worthwhile.

We have to be flexible, willing to change our mind every now and again. To accept a new direction, or new "facts on the ground." But most of all – we have to keep trusting our own unconquerable spirit.

I'm so happy to be sharing these few thoughts with you sitting at the wheel of a very elegant, very beautiful machine. My hat goes off to all those people, probably in many different parts of the world, who helped to make this beautiful computer possible. My hat goes off to all those gifted and kind people who, on the telephone for the most part, have helped me get my new computer set up and running properly.

CHAPTER 7

Who Could be Knocking at the Door at This Hour?

> *"All that is required to realize the self is to be still. What can be easier than that?"*
> – Ramana Maharshi.

The front door bell rang one evening around six or so. Then as I was making my way to the door there was an insistent knock. Goodness, what's this? I thought. It's rare for someone to visit us around that time, and as I opened the door I wondered if it might be a solicitation of some kind.

A young woman was there. She had a sweet, although troubled expression on her face. I had never seen her before, but quickly registered that she didn't want to give me any religious tracts or suchlike.

"I'm sorry to trouble you," she said, "but have you seen a small black poodle in the street? I've lost him and I'm trying to find him."

I couldn't really help. I hadn't seen any sign of such a creature.

But it was such a very sweet moment as I commiserated with this young woman and we shared a moment of mutual humanity, love and compassion. Before I closed the door I said I was sure she would find her dog. She smiled a little wistfully and went on her way. I'm sure I will never see her again, and will never know what happened to her small black poodle.

We tend to take everyday encounters with other people fairly casually, for the most part, understandably so. We have things to do and places to go, as my wife JoAnn likes to say. But there is an opportunity present any time we meet someone to see them in a true light – the light of God, the light of Eternal Love.

CHAPTER 8

Is Happiness Hiding in Plain Sight?

> *"We can smile, breathe, walk, and eat our meals in a way that allows us to be in touch with the abundance of happiness that is available. We are very good at preparing to live, but not very good at living. We know how to sacrifice ten years for a diploma and we are willing to work very hard to get a job, a car, a house, and so on. But we have difficulty remembering that we are alive in the present moment, the only moment there is for us to be alive."*
> – Thich Nhat Hanh

Every once in a while, in my exchanges with my wife JoAnn, I succeed in saying something that is funny – funny enough anyway to provoke spontaneous laughter in her.

I've noticed how at a certain point, when she has been laughing awhile, she pauses and says, "Oh heck." It's been going on for years. I realize how much I love hearing these two simple little words in this context.

I've also become more consciously aware of something else that happens when she laughs. She always finishes her laugh with a warble – don't know how else to describe it – a unique sound that comes from somewhere deep in her throat and sounds like happiness itself humming with joy.

I shared a joke with a doctor one time. We were talking on the phone, and he was apologizing for the fact that he was croaking because of a bad cold.

As the conversation came to a close I couldn't resist it. I said, "I've got one or two good medical books here, Dr. Thom. Maybe I could find some advice that would help with your cold?"

I'm afraid my jokes don't always work. But I think this one did, because he began wheezing with laughter. It may sound strange. But there was as much happiness in me in that simple little moment as when I walked up the gangway of a Holland America cruise ship a few years ago at the start of a Caribbean cruise with JoAnn.

Perhaps the expectations we load on to "big" events work against us sometimes? Reality has a difficult time living up to them?

In any event, I find more and more that gold – the gold of joy, happiness and love – is in the little everyday moments of life. It's "hiding in plain sight." All it needs is our attention.

CHAPTER 9

The Magic of Synchronicity

> *"I am open to the guidance of synchronicity, and do not let expectations hinder my path."*
> – The Dalai Lama

I've been called "the world's oldest, newest blogger," and I assert with confidence that one of the joys of aging is developing a greater appreciation for the mystery Carl Jung called synchronicity.

Synchronicity touched my life in an extraordinary way and I'm still drunk with the happiness of it all.

I had been invited to a private school called the HomeSpun Academy in Loveland, Colorado, to speak about a book I self-published a few years ago entitled *The Raven Who Spoke with God.*

The book is a fable about integrity and the “hero's journey.” I wrote it at a Starbucks soon after moving to Denver to marry JoAnn. It describes how a young raven named Joshua feels a sense of destiny in life and follows his mission regardless of the many challenges that confront him.

Goodness knows, I didn’t plan it this way. But the book came out on 9/11. It was translated into 11 foreign-language editions during the years following 9/11, but more recently it seemed to me it had run its course. Since we were planning to move to Denver I decided to give away some copies to Habitat before we moved.

As I say, I thought my book had reached the end of its natural life span. Little did I know that life had other ideas for *The Raven Who Spoke with God.*

The principal of the HomeSpun Academy, Beth Sowders, saw a box of the books for sale for a few dollars at Habitat and decided to buy them.

But the box of books remained unopened on a shelf until August 2010, when Beth, facing a big challenge in her life, decided to read a copy. As she told me during my visit – the book changed her life.

Enrollment at HomeSpun had dropped and she was wondering whether it was the right thing to continue her work with the school. The story of a young raven who was true to his mission despite major challenges inspired her so much she knew it was the right thing to keep the school going.

"By the end of the book, I couldn't stop crying," Sowders said to her students when she introduced me to them. "God showed me my destiny is to be a teacher."

She had made the book part of the school curriculum. So when I arrived at the school I had the immense pleasure of meeting a group of students aged about 10 to 18 who loved the book and had been inspired by it to think more deeply about their lives.

Each of the students wrote me a note of appreciation.

Said one: "This book was very inspirational to me in some things that I was going through. I enjoyed having a character like Joshua, who goes through a very hard time at the beginning, but it got better along the way. I'm really happy that you wrote this book, because it showed me that even in the hardest of times God is always there to help you get through it."

Synchronicity is an aspect of grace, as far as I'm concerned. I believe that like grace, it is always ready to bring happiness and healing into our lives – but of course we have to play our part.

We have to be open to its guidance, as the Dalai Lama points out. We have to listen to the little nudges that life brings to us, and act on the wisdom of our own heart.

Meeting Beth Sowders and her students was one of the greatest joys and fulfillments of my life for I had always hoped my raven book would help to remind people of any age of the unique destiny we each have to fulfill.

But suppose Beth had not bought the box of books I had more or less abandoned? Or suppose she simply left the book unread? Then the synchronicity I experienced would never have happened.

And I would never have met a wonderful group of young people whose passion and love for truth will inspire me for a long time.

Don't be too quick to give up on your dreams – synchronicity can touch your life at any time and at any age in ways you perhaps could never imagine.

CHAPTER 10

How a Wooden Sword Helped Me Heal

> *"For me, singing sad songs often has a way of healing a situation. It gets the hurt out in the open into the light, out of the darkness."*
> – Reba McEntire

A wooden sword sits on a window ledge in my little office. It's a replica of a Chinese sword from the age of the samurai and it has quite a story to tell.

Not so long ago, let's say 20-25 years ago, there were three constants in my life. At least, I thought they were constants. It certainly would never have entered my head that one day one of these constants might cease to exist – let alone that all three might simply vanish and pass away within a few short years.

But that's what happened. First, I lost my spiritual mentor, the man I had loved and followed faithfully for more than 35 years, when he died unexpectedly in January 1988. Then my wonderful wife Joy, to whom I had been married for 25 years, also died suddenly in December 1991.

Finally, on a cold fall morning in October 1994, I said goodbye forever to the spiritual community that had been my home in British Columbia for 36 years. I had no alternative. The community didn't exist anymore. It had gradually disintegrated as more and more people left following our leader's death.

This is where my wooden sword comes into the picture. Of course, it wasn't the sword itself that helped me heal. It was what it symbolized to me.

My entire world had shattered. I was in a state of numbness, denial, and terrible grief. I felt I was on the edge of an abyss, with virtually no money and no prospects that I could see – what was I going to do?

Thank God, the first step was clear enough. It was to go to Vancouver, 300 miles to the south, where my son, Durwin, lived. I will always be so thankful for the friendship and support he offered to me, and offers to this day. A day or two after arriving in

Vancouver to begin what seemed the hopeless task of rebuilding my life, I had a sudden impulse. "Go to Chinatown and buy a wooden sword," a voice said to me in my heart. "It will be a symbol of the warrior spirit that you will need to handle this situation you're in."

I remember quite vividly taking a bus to Chinatown and then, because this was Vancouver, getting soaked as I walked for several blocks in heavy rain looking for a suitable sword. Finally I found one, and in the difficult, confusing days that followed, this wooden sword did indeed help me navigate the challenge before me.

I mention this little story because perhaps in these difficult times a physical symbol of some kind can be helpful or perhaps already is being helpful to you too?

On this same theme, my wife JoAnn was telling me the other day how for many years she was troubled by the notion that her mother loved her sister more than she loved her. One day JoAnn was looking at a portrait of herself taken when she was about 8 years old, when she suddenly realized that this idea she had carried with her for so long simply wasn't true.

She realized, as she looked at the old picture of herself, how happy she looked, and how nicely dressed she was – and what nice Shirley Temple curls her mother had put in her hair. She realized her mother really did love her and a burden lifted in her.

CHAPTER 11

How Ritual Can Bless Your Life

> *"An early-morning walk is a blessing for the whole day."*
> – Henry David Thoreau

Ritual covers a much bigger territory than you may have realized. And while, like anything, ritual can be used wrongly, it can also be used rightly – in very practical ways – to give us courage and comfort, to inspire us, and help us meet the challenges that life brings.

In my early 20s, I ran into a very difficult time in my life when I returned home to London to "settle down" after spending some time in Southern Rhodesia (now Zimbabwe) and New Zealand. I felt confused and alienated from my British middle class background even as an inner voice proclaimed loudly and fiercely that there was a true purpose for my life and I needed to get busy and find it.

The day before leaving Auckland to sail home to England I had bought a book called *Leaves of Grass*, by Walt Whitman. The little book "jumped" into my hand apparently by chance in a bookshop and went with me everywhere for two years.

I read a little bit of Whitman every day. The book was with me when I went to work as a reporter on the Daily Express newspaper in London. It was with me when I went sailing in my small boat on the Essex coast. It was still with me when at the age of 23 I went to British Columbia to find a new life.

Then one day I didn't feel the need to read Walt Whitman any more. My "ritual" came to an end as naturally and spontaneously as it had begun. I still loved Walt but I didn't need his help any longer.

Rituals give structure to our lives. They give us a track to run on. The key, it seems to me, is being flexible, not afraid to follow new routines, particularly when they arise spontaneously in our lives, and not afraid to let them go when they have served their purpose.

Here are a few rituals that bring joy to my life:

1. Abdominal breathing first thing in the morning and last thing at night helps bring calm and focus.
2. Working out at the gym makes me feel strong.
3. Telling JoAnn how wonderful she is makes me feel good.
4. Going to the coffee shop in the afternoon gets me away from my little office and gives me a chance to read and connect with other people, or perhaps not do anything at all.
5. Appreciating little moments opens my mind and heart to life's magic.
6. A glass of wine on the porch in the evening lets me commune with Nature and passers-by – and perhaps pat their dogs.
7. Listening to birds soothes my soul.
8. Watching the evening news connects me with the world.

CHAPTER 12

Sometimes Simple and Familiar Is Good

> *"Sometimes at the best moments a single word or a look is enough."*
> – Honore De Balzac

I was feeling two conflicting emotions at the same time this morning. Ever happen to you? The adventurous side of me, which worries sometimes that it isn't getting enough expression in my life, was saying, "Look, it's Sunday, you've been working hard, do something bold like going for a hike in the mountains so you know you're really alive."

But another part of me wasn't so sure. It just didn't seem to want to do anything too exciting or dramatic at all. I went and sat for a few minutes with JoAnn, always a good idea if I need a little help clarifying my mind about something.

She was working on a new sewing project, and of course said, as she always does, that I must decide for myself what to do. But she suggested that the past few days had been particularly exciting and challenging for me – working on a new book project that could possibly make a difference to our lives if it all works out — and perhaps what I really needed was simply to relax and let things settle down a bit.

I decided to gas up the car, a fairly safe step. But then, as I finished filling up the tank, I thought to myself, "Why not just go for a walk by the creek and be nourished and soothed by something simple that won't need a lot of exertion?"

So I drove home, walked down the little hill at the back of our property and sat down on a bench to listen to the sweet sound of the creek. In just a few moments a chickadee – one of my favorite birds – began to sing, and I saw a blue jay, the first one I've seen this year.

I met friendly people. I met friendly dogs. I sat on a rock beside a small waterfall. I saw daffodils getting ready to bloom. It was a simple little adventure. And yet I knew it was just right. It was what I needed to do.

I felt fulfilled, and rested. I felt nourished.

Sometimes life demands that we be bold, and daring, and take a huge step into the unknown regardless of any uncertainty or anxiety we may feel, and no matter what the cost may be. There is no guarantee at all things will work out the way we hope they will — but we sense deep in our bones that our very destiny is at stake.

And sometimes simple and familiar is good. Oh, so good. May we have the wisdom to know what really needs to be done in any particular situation, and may our lives prosper because of it.

CHAPTER 13

Something Calling to You

> *"Let nothing disturb thee, nothing affright thee. All things are changing, God changeth not."*
> – St Teresa of Avila

There is something in you and me that is not troubled in the least by the various challenges and upheavals of our lives. No matter what has happened to you – or is happening to you now – it is untouched and unharmed by any of it.

Good times come and good times go. You meet someone who makes your life complete, or maybe you lose someone you loved with a passion. You achieve a dream you were following for many years, or perhaps you wake up one morning and realize your life is empty and always has been.

But this silent presence within you is unmoved by any of it. It shines like the sun. It's at peace. It doesn't move, it doesn't change. It's not going somewhere, and it didn't come from somewhere either. It's like a seed planted in the earth, waiting to be born into a flower, or a tree, or a new world. And the only word I can think to describe it is love.

This love that is in us was never born, and will never die. It is the source of everything but here's the interesting thing. It has never once lost its faith in you. It knows why you are here, and amid all the trials and tribulations of your life, it has never once deviated in its love for you.

Shh. Be still. Listen. Can you hear something calling to you amid the hustle and bustle of your daily routine? It's love, your own true nature, and it wants to be free. It wants you to be free too. It wants to come out of hiding and set the whole world free.

Its time has come and it's on the move. It has its own agenda for this world and it doesn't really care about our political persuasions or cultural persuasions or religious persuasions. It's love, and you'd better believe it is not going to be defeated.

CHAPTER 14

Top 10 Ways to Be Unhappy

> *"Success is not the key to happiness. Happiness is the key to success. If you love what you are doing, you will be successful."*
> – Albert Schweitzer

I've got a brilliant idea. There is a lot of information out there about how to be happy – how to be more successful, how to find inner peace, how to squeeze more joy and satisfaction out of life, and so on.

But some people simply enjoy being miserable and want to keep it that way. Where can *they* turn for help and advice?

To help fill this void I offer the following simple, proven, 10-step program guaranteed to bring greater unhappiness and pain into anyone's life.

1. Never be still

Never, ever be still. Keep yourself busy and distracted at all times. You have to realize that stillness is your number one enemy, because if you give it half a chance it will open a door to undreamed-of joy and bliss. I don't care if this is a conscious realization or an unconscious one – just as long as you refuse to be still under any circumstance.

My advice? Do whatever it takes. Go on a trip. Buy a new scarf. Get a new car. Get a new husband or wife. Get rid of your present husband or wife. And so on and so forth.

2. Never question your beliefs

Never, NEVER question any of your beliefs or prejudices. This can be very dangerous, because it may open your mind to a new sense of the limitless beauty and potential of life. In fact, the more I think about this step, the more I realize that it is just as important as the first step. In any case, just realize that if you dare to question any of your beliefs in this time of rapid change and transformation it may have creative consequences – the very result you are trying to avoid.

3. Stay away from dogs

Be very careful to have no contact whatsoever with animals, particularly dogs. This is a big mistake that many misery lovers frequently make. Dogs, you see – and many other animals, not to mention birds and trees and whatnot – can make us happy without saying a word. I'm just warning you in the strongest possible terms – stay away from dogs.

4. Watch out for babies

The above applies to babies. It's true that babies can sometimes make a person irritated or angry. But it's a well-known fact that a baby can change our mood for the better in an instant – even more effectively than dogs can. Babies are a special problem deserving of a fuller treatment than is possible to me in this brief report.

5. Repeat this mantra every day

At the beginning of every day, repeat this mantra three times. It's most effective when spoken aloud, but if circumstances prevent that, it is still effective when you merely repeat the words in your head. Say to yourself with as much conviction as possible: "This is going to be a terrible day. I know it's going to be a terrible day."

6. Congratulate yourself on your misery

   At the end of the day, take a moment to look back and congratulate yourself how miserable you were.

7. Distract yourself from the present moment

   This is the most important step in the program. Distract yourself as much as possible from the present moment. TV is a very effective tool in this regard. I guarantee that the more you can train yourself to do this the more miserable you will be.

8. Remember you are better than anyone else

   Make it a guiding principle in your life to remember that you are a little bit better than anyone else. One or two exceptions are okay. But remind yourself of this every day. Supermarkets are a good place to practise. Subways are equally good.

   This is the surest way to maintain a gnawing sense of unhappiness and loneliness that I know of.

9. Be careful what books you read

   Be very careful what books you read. Read only books that support your views. By the same token, carefully censor what TV talk-show hosts you watch, what radio stations you listen to, and so on.

10. Never allow hope to take root

    Finally, if you really want to remain enmeshed in a bottomless pit of despair never allow that ridiculous notion called "Hope" to take root in your heart. It can be *very* dangerous.

Please let me know how this plan works for you. Good luck to you.

CHAPTER 15

The True Gift of Christmas

> *Who is more foolish, the child afraid of the dark or the man afraid of the light?*
> – Maurice Freehill

Jesus, it is written, came to earth to bring a gift. The gift of light. The gift of love. The gift of truth.

You and I also came to earth to bring a gift – the same gift, the gift of our own true nature, the gift of our own compassionate, loving spirit, the true birthright of each one of us.

The spirit of love that shone so brightly in Jesus and also rightly finds a home in us has no part in aging. It is as fresh and radiant and life-giving in this moment as it was at any moment in the past.

It never loses its luster. It is unchanged from age to age. Only the forms through which it finds expression experience what we call birth and death.

We are spiritual beings. And if Christmas has meaning, which I believe it certainly does, potentially at least, it is this. It is an opportunity to honor and give thanks for the brave, wise, compassionate spirit that was in Jesus – and that we are privileged to share and carry forward in our own lives.

CHAPTER 16

9 Steps to a New Life

> *"Don't go around saying the world owes you a living. The world owes you nothing. It was here first."*
> – Mark Twain

One day a reader of my blog sent me a message saying he was in the middle of a messy divorce that also affected a number of children.

"I'm having a difficult time dealing with the rejection and being all alone in an empty apartment with my clothes and laptop," he said. "Do you have any advice on how I can let go, rebuild and move on to a meaningful life?"

I thought about this request and came up with the following ideas and suggestions.

1. Let yourself feel your feelings

This is a very hard thing for most people to do, at least when the feelings are painful, frightening, and hard to bear. We've been conditioned – at least I was – to try to escape unpleasant feelings. We suppress them. We try to drown them in work, play, alcohol, sex, a new car, a new house or some other distraction.

But I have found in my own life after quite a few traumas that the quickest route to healing and happiness – in fact the only route – is to let ourselves feel our feelings at all costs. If we do, we will make an extraordinary discovery. Any feeling, no matter how awful, or how delightful, has a beginning and an end.

The payoff, if we take this immensely challenging step, is that it opens the door to a real miracle. We become aware of something that does not have a beginning or an end – our own true presence, untroubled and undisturbed by any of the vicissitudes of our life.

2. Create a daily ritual

   Giving yourself permission to experience your feelings is not "soft," or weak. It has nothing to do with being a victim. It takes real strength to feel what you are feeling without either wallowing in it or trying to escape from it.

   So here's a suggestion. Create a daily ritual, or ceremony for yourself. It won't be forever, just until you begin to feel some relief and confidence. Take 15 minutes a day (adjust as you wish – perhaps in the evening) when the only thing you do is sit quietly in a chair and feel whatever comes up in your heart.

   You may be surprised by the power of this ritual. It not only opens a door to reconnect with yourself at a deeper level, it also begins to create some boundaries. For example, if painful feelings come up during the day – tell them they will have to wait a little. They will have their chance to be heard later at such and such a time.

3. Do whatever comforts you and enlivens you

One of my lifelines, when I was deep, deep down in an abyss of despair was going to my favorite coffee shop each afternoon. I was very religious about this. The world might be falling apart beneath my feet, but the coffee shop didn't seem to be fazed by my tribulations at all.

The people who served me coffee were as cheerful as ever. And just being aware of other people being "normal" – living "normal" lives as they went about their business, sipping their lattes, telling stories, discussing business, or working hard at their computer was very therapeutic.

It helped to relieve my sense of isolation and reminded me that no matter what was going on in my own life, I was part of the larger family of humankind and there was a big blessing in that.

4. Do something for someone else

Do something for someone else. This piece of wisdom has been around for a long time, but this is because it works. It connects us immediately with the kindness, compassion and love that is the core of our own being.

And by the way, it doesn't have to be something big or spectacular. Just smiling at a neighbor or a lady serving you in a supermarket will do it. Little steps to serenity and well-being are just as important as big steps – perhaps even more important.

5. Perhaps you can volunteer somewhere?

   Along this line, perhaps you can volunteer somewhere, and help other people in that way?

6. Stay close to Nature

   Staying close to Nature is helps keep us grounded in times of trouble. Find a stream and listen to it. Look at a tree and admire it. Or how about getting a dog?

   JoAnn and I don't have a dog, but we live in a town house complex in which quite a few people do have dogs. I find patting a neighbor's dog is very therapeutic. The dog usually enjoys it too.

7. Let go of your wife

   Let go of your wife. As long as you are estranged from each other she's the last person you should look to right now for any kind of help or useful conversation. Give her the dignity and space to pursue her own path at this juncture in her life – while you do the same.

8. Get regular exercise

   Exercise has been a true lifesaver for me and countless others in times of trouble. Scientists have discovered that exercise helps burn up stress hormones – amazing, isn't it?

9. Forgive your ex-wife

   Lastly, forgive your ex-wife. This may be a hard thing to do, especially now. But it's critical not only for her but for you too.

CHAPTER 17

Just Sit Quietly and See What Happens

"All of man's difficulties are caused by his inability to sit quietly in a room."
– Blaise Pascal

Here's a true story that happened recently. I like to do the right thing on Sunday and make breakfast for JoAnn and me. Mind you, I only really have one culinary skill – but it's a good one, handed down through many generations of British ancestors.

I'm very good at boiling eggs. So as usual yesterday, JoAnn and I each had a boiled egg and toast – the eggs boiled, though I say so myself, to perfection. Nothing unusual so far, right? We ate our breakfast, and I put everything away properly because there's no point in only doing half a job, is there?

I had planned to go for a nice walk after breakfast, but after finishing up in the kitchen a strong compulsion arose in me just to sit down in my favorite chair and be still.

I try to follow my inner "nudges," so I put the walk on one side and sat down obediently in my chair. Immediately, a thought came up, "You could read the newspaper." But reading the paper didn't feel right.

With no previous intention on my part I disappeared, as it were, into a "thought free zone." For about an hour, I simply sat in my chair, utterly surrendered to an experience of happiness and joy that in one sense felt very new and in another sense very familiar.

It was like being bathed by love, while sitting in a fountain of bliss. Once in awhile a thought came up, but I just wasn't interested. The joy and peace that I was experiencing was so beautiful, complete, and compelling.

We tend to be afraid of stillness. Being busy is what keeps us sane, after all, or so we think. But remarkable things happen when we give ourselves permission to sit quietly. Many years ago my wife, an intuitive lady, was sitting in her favorite chair in her small town home in Denver wondering, "Is this all I'm supposed be doing with my life?"

Suddenly she had a momentary sense that someone was sitting in the empty chair across the room. It was such an extraordinary experience that it disoriented her for a few moments. Then, almost immediately, the phone started to ring. It was me, in Vancouver, also feeling a bit stuck, wondering what my next move in life was supposed to be.

I had never met JoAnn, but I knew who she was because we had belonged to the same spiritual group for many years. I was planning to visit Colorado to attend a retreat and I thought, "Why not call JoAnn and see if we can have a coffee together?" That's how we got together. We married a year later.

Give yourself permission to be still for a few moments and see what happens. You may be amazed.

CHAPTER 18

Something You Can Trust All Your Life

> *"We run, not because we think it is doing us good, but because we enjoy it and cannot help ourselves. The more restricted our society and work become, the more necessary it will be to find some outlet for this craving for freedom. No one can say, 'You must not run faster than this, or jump higher than that.' The human spirit is indomitable."*
>
> – Roger Bannister

The last time I saw my Dad was when he saw me off at the train station at Eastbourne, a seaside town on the south coast of England. We said goodbye at the ticket barrier, but as I was starting to walk to the train a small voice inside me said, "Turn around and watch your Dad."

Dad was 94. He lived alone in a small ground-floor flat directly across from his favorite pub in a village called Pevensey Bay, not far from Eastbourne. I had come over from British Columbia to visit him. He died less than a year later.

As I stood at the barrier and watched Dad walk slowly and deliberately toward the exit, I marveled at how upright he was, and I felt a quickening of love and admiration for him I had never felt before in my whole life.

He was 6'3". He was careful, and yet so unutterably proud, in the way he walked. Straight as a ramrod. Upright as a redwood. Careful, though, not to take too big of a step. Careful in the way he used his stick to help him. Careful not to trip or fall. But never losing his poise.

What I saw bursting through him with each step he took was his indomitable spirit. A spirit tried in peace and war. In 75 years of brave journalism – to quote a commemorative silver plate he received toward the end of his life from fellow London journalists — and in a million other ways.

He was as brave at 94 as he was when he was 60, listening to a judge sentence him to 6 months in prison for refusing to betray his principles and

Left to Right: my Aunt Kathleen, my wonderful wife, JoAnn, and Dad

reveal his sources to a government spy tribunal. His quick jokes, a specialty of his, didn't diminish in quality as far as I could see, and he remained as gallant as ever to the ladies. It impressed the heck out of my wife the first time they met when he insisted on carrying her coat.

In this world in which we live it seems as if there is less and less upon which we can really depend. Jobs quit on us. Relationships quit on us. Institutions quit on us. Sometimes friendships quit on us. Some argue government is quitting on them.

Cars are quite well-known for quitting on people, too, though in fairness to automakers it does seem as if they are doing a better job these days.

But there is something you can trust that will never quit on you, and it is your own unconquerable spirit. The idea of quitting never enters its head. And its love never fails.

I feel Dad's indomitable spirit present with me more strongly than ever, cheering me on, shall I say. And with all his flaws, and all my flaws, I'm glad he was my Dad.

CHAPTER 19

100 Steps to Grace

> *As in nature, as in art, so in grace; it is rough treatment that gives souls, as well as stones, their luster.*
> – Thomas Guthrie.

I wrote these thoughts down in a "flow of consciousness"one day. I hope they will give you some ideas about ways to create new happiness and joy in your life.

1. Pick up a stone and admire it.
2. After you put the stone down look at your hand and admire that. Have you ever seen a more beautiful creation?
3. Put a hand on your belly and do some abdominal breathing, with only your belly moving.

4. My dad, who was in great shape until he died at 95, used to make a point of thinking of something pleasant before he went to sleep. Try it, see if it works for you.

5. Read the 23rd Psalm.

6. Read a verse or two from Gitanjali, by Rabindranath Tagore.

7. Does life seem so transitory sometimes? Consider the possibility that at the core of your being you are timeless and changeless.

8. Look at a photo of your Mom and honor her.

9. Don't look to the world for a sense of importance – look within, to your own being.

10. Look up at the sky.

11. Consider the timeless words: "My yoke is easy, my burden is light."

12. Be still.

13. Be still some more.

14. Listen to your own inner voice and trust it.

15. Say "thank you" and really mean it.

16. Consider the possibility that you don't have to look for happiness because who you truly are is already happy.

17. Do the thing your mind says it doesn't want to do.

18. Trust life.

19. Don't let thoughts dictate your life.

20. Why see thoughts as an enemy? Notice that thoughts come and go but the truth of you is always here.

21. Listen to the sweet sound of running water.

22. Be of equal grace to all.

23. Thank your spouse or partner for the many gifts they bring to your life.

24. Trust that life is good and if you play your part everything will unfold as it should.

25. Find some ducks somewhere and admire them.

26. Remember it's never too late to change your mind.

27. Remember it's never too late to be happy.

28. Don't keep your happiness to yourself. Spread it around.

29. Wondering what to do as you age? Consider starting a blog. Remember, it’s never too late to be a blogger.

30. Don't close up when strong feelings come. I tried it for a long, long time, and it doesn't work. Let yourself feel your feelings no matter how painful they may be.

31. Discover paradox. Accept paradox. Realize that true nature is strong and also gentle.

32. It's never too late to get in shape. Consider going to a gym. You may find it's a lifesaver.

33. Spend more time with Nature.

34. Admire the beauty of the sky and remind yourself that it simply reflects your own beauty.

35. The sky simply reflects back to us the spaciousness of our true nature as a deer or flower or robin remind us of the oneness of creation.

36. Never pass up an opportunity to pat a dog – unless, of course, you suspect it might be best left alone.

37. If someone has helped you, or done their best to help you, make sure they know how much you appreciate them.

38. If you are in despair remember that on the other side of despair is joy.

39. It's the joy of our own true nature, untouched and unchanged by any of the adversities of life.

40. We come into this world with a unique gift to give. It’s the gift of our own presence.

41. Take time to listen to the sounds around you, your own breathing, the clock on the wall, some passing geese, or the laughter of a child.

42. Don't only listen to external sounds. Listen also to the wisdom of your own spirit speaking to you in the quietness of your heart.

43. Be brave.

44. Be patient. Patience is one of the greatest gifts of the universe. As long as you are doing the best you know how in this moment, don’t be concerned about the future. It will take care of itself.

45. Take pleasure in little things.

46. Take pleasure in the chickadee and her unique little cries.

47. Take pleasure in the sight of a woman enjoying her grandchildren.

48. Give thanks for the gift your own physical body has given you.

49. Is your body getting old, or having troubles at the moment? Acknowledge how faithful it has been through the years.

50. Don't be afraid if you lose something precious. There is one thing you can never lose – your own boundless nature.

51. Do something silly. Whatever your age, come out to play.

52. Sing the next time you vacuum the house.

53. Just because you have done something a certain way before doesn't mean you have to keep doing it the same way.

54. Life is a victorious experience when we live it with a victorious spirit.

55. There are riches and joys waiting to be revealed that we have never even dreamed of yet.

56. Persistence is part of your true nature. There is always more persistence available to us.

57. Life is a trickster though. There are times when persistence is NOT called for.

58. Remember Gibran. “Who bakes bread without love bakes a bitter bread that feeds but half man's hunger.”

59. When in doubt, smile.

60. Do some more abdominal breathing right now.

61. It's good to be whole. The truth is, you are already whole.

62. Ever think about looking into Chi Gung? It has many gifts to give, especially as we age.

63. A wonderful resource on Chi Gung is *The Way of Energy* by Master Lam Kam Chuen.

64. Be kind to yourself.

65. Some words I say to myself once in a while: "Everything is going to be all right."

66. “It’s all right,” my Mum said in the early days of WWII as bombs fell all around our apartment block in central London and the entire building swayed back and forth beneath us.

67. Never forget the sea, and its wonderful healing energy.

68. Just listening to the roar and rumble of the sea will uplift the lowliest spirit.

69. The sea is primeval like the lion and the forest, and you and me.

70. Stop and listen to the hum of the universe in your ear.

71. Stop and note the magnificence of the universe in a fine painting, or in a mountain, or in a brightly colored butterfly.

72. Be true to yourself. Honor yourself. Above all, listen to the voice of your own being in the quietness of your heart.

73. Feel the skin of your left hand. Isn't it a miracle?

74. Pick a blade of grass this summer and stick it between your teeth like you did when you were young.

75. My favorite picture hangs above my computer. It shows a young fox at rest on a mound of earth with a piece of grass in his teeth, eyes shut and face aglow with bliss.

76. Bliss is our true nature. Don't let go of your bliss, follow it wherever it takes you.

77. Don’t be too quick to form an opinion of someone – it takes time to really get to know another person.

78. Reach out and try something new.

79. Who are you, really? Suppose you are an aspect of Eternal Love finding expression through human form? Our forms come and go – but the love that you truly are has neither beginning nor end.

80. "Love never fails." Were more beautiful words ever written?

81. Where are the limits of love? Does it have any limits?

82. Love is not bound by time. I just thought of my mother, long gone, and felt a closeness with her that is as strong now as it ever was.

83. If love transcends time, perhaps it also transcends space?

84. If the truth of your being is love, and you get on a plane and go somewhere, do you really go anywhere?

85. Perhaps, when we think we travel, or move from here to there, we are fooling ourselves?

86. Perhaps the truth of you has not moved at all?

87. Perhaps here is the secret of true peace?

88. Got to say a word in support of ravens. I love ravens. I'm so glad that the townhome complex where JoAnn and I live has a resident flock of ravens we can listen to and watch every day.

89. Don't only look for happiness in big things like a relationship, or a trip to Hawaii, or Bali. Look for joy in little moments like going for a walk, drinking a cup of tea, or chatting with a friend.

90. Bliss is a gift from the universe. It's who we are. It's part of our divine nature.

91. Let the joy that is already inside you express through you to bless your life and the lives of others.

92. Joy is our true name. It was our name before we came into this world, and it will still be our name when we say goodbye to our earthly body that has been our home and friend in this life.

93. The more responsibility you take for your own life the happier you will be.

94. The more responsibility we take for our planet the happier it will be.

95. Joy and freedom. Freedom and joy. Such beautiful words, aren't they?

96. I'm writing this post in a suburb of Denver in sunny Colorado. Wherever you are, and wherever you live, I send best wishes to you.

97. We are not as separate from one another as we may think.

98. You are part of a beautiful, intelligent whole.

99. You are loved by this whole.

100. Trust your own unconquerable spirit.

CHAPTER 20

It's Never Too Late to Be a Handyman

> *"You cannot teach old dogs new tricks."*
> – Joseph Chamberlain

It's never too late to be a handyman, I learned the other day. My dad was a great journalist, but went through his entire life hardly knowing what a screwdriver was. It was like he prided himself on not being very good with tools — and I grew up with the same approach.

So here's what happened. I had just finished watering the bushes in the front of our townhome when JoAnn asked me to hose down the front door and windows. Which I did. About 30 minutes later, as we were having lunch, the front doorbell rang. "Who can that be," we wondered. I went to the front door, but there was nobody there.

After lunch it was time for our afternoon rest, a wonderful survival strategy for people of a certain age. We had just got comfortable when the doorbell rang again. So of course I got up to answer – but once again, to my surprise, there was no one there.

To cut a long story short, the front doorbell continued to ring every hour or two – with never a visitor in sight – until finally, around five o'clock, I realized I had to do something about the situation. "We don't want to be listening to the front doorbell all night do we," I told JoAnn.

Presumably spraying water all over the doorbell had made it angry. But while the urgency of our situation was beginning to dawn on me (ha-ha) the problem was, what was I going to do about it? My first thought was, call someone for help. But it was Memorial Day. I couldn't call an electrician or a professional handyman, could I?

I summoned my British spirit and took a bold step. "It won't hurt to take the cover off the doorbell panel in the hallway and have a look at it, will it?" I said to JoAnn.

I got something to stand on, removed the cover and inspected the mechanism. I saw it included two wires, each fastened down on separate little plates by a screw.

Here is where I am quite proud of myself. It occurred to me that these wires obviously played an important part in making the whole thing work. And if I could somehow detach them the doorbell that was threatening our peace of mind and would definitely sabotage our sleep might have a hard time ringing, right?

I went and grabbed a screwdriver from my toolbox. Yes, I do have a toolbox. It isn't very big, about a foot long by 6 inches wide, but there are a few things in it that can be useful, like some string, a pair of pliers etc.

Just for a moment, a thought crossed my mind, "Is there a chance I might get an electric shock?" But I dismissed it and JoAnn was actually very impressed when I loosened the two screws I've told you about and pried the wires loose.

"Don't see how it can work now," I said smugly. And indeed that is how it worked out. In fact the doorbell is still blissfully quiet as I write this post. Dad would be proud of me I'm sure. Perhaps there's a handyman in all of us just waiting to come out and go to work?

CHAPTER 21

Resilience Is Your Ally As You Age

> *"There's no such thing as ruining your life. Life's a pretty resilient thing, it turns out."*
> – Sophie Kinsella

How vital is the power of resilience. And how it warms my heart to read a story showing the power of resilience at work. A story like the one I was reading in the Denver Post the other morning.

A young Denver Broncos quarterback named Tim Tebow – scorned by local sportswriters after performing poorly in one or two opening games – answered his critics with a brilliant performance against the Oakland Raiders on Sunday.

I'm a Brit. My favorite game is, or was, soccer. But resilience doesn't recognize cultural or national boundaries.

Resilience is part of our true nature and it is particularly important as we age. It is your ally, no matter what your age. It is there for you always, unperturbed and untroubled by any of the challenges or troubles of your life.

Even if you ignore it, or consider it of no importance, resilience is still your ally, ready in a flash to help you heal from a disappointment or trauma, be it large or small. All you have to do is to be quiet for a moment and ask and the power of resilience will be there to help you just as it helped Tim Tebow.

Does a voice in your head from who knows where rear its ugly head sometimes and say, "My life has been in vain." Or, "I am confused, and don't know what to do." Or, "Why isn't my life more interesting?" Or, "You're getting older, you're not relevant any more."

I have found in my life that while the voice of old habits and conditioning can seem strong at times, the power of resilience is stronger.

If you are still, and listen, resilience will always bring you back on course. It will give you strength. It will remind you of your own unconquerable spirit. It will dispel the voices of discouragement and despair and flood the windows of your soul with light. It will give you new confidence in myself.

How thankful I am for the gift of resilience. It is timeless, and unaffected by any of the challenges of our lives.

CHAPTER 22

Moving With the Rhythms of Life

> *"I may not have gone where I intended to go, but I think I have ended up where I intended to be."*
> – Douglas Adams

Life tosses some hard things at us at times. But I have discovered, like so many, that there's a rhythm in the way life works.

Yes, difficult, wrenching times come to us all. But if we persist through our challenges, and trust our own unconquerable spirit, we are led, with absolute certainty, to a deeper experience of peace and well-being that perhaps would have been unimaginable to us before.

Take the time I set out on my first cruise in a small sailboat from Victoria, B.C., many years ago, for example.

I had a preview of the way this remarkable rhythm works when a strong headwind blew up and took me by surprise.

It was a scary time. Yet less than two hours later, the wind died away and I entered the safety of a beautiful cove. The water was as smooth and calm as velvet as I sailed deeper into the cove with the barest hint of a breeze. I was overwhelmed with the magic and peace of the moment.

There was no other boat in sight. There was just me, the smooth surface over which I was gliding, and the stars that were beginning to appear in the night sky.

I had never felt such peace in my whole life. I felt as if God himself had reached down to bless me, and I knew that my passion to discover the truth of life was not in vain.

There is a place of perfect peace in each one of us that nothing can harm or disturb. It is waiting for you in this very moment.

CHAPTER 23

You Can Heal Your Past

> *"Simply touching a difficult memory with some slight willingness to heal begins to soften the holding and tension around it."*
> – Stephen Levine

Sometimes as we move bravely through our days we carry a burden from our past that ruins the quality of our life now and prevents us from experiencing the blessed life that is our birthright. But suppose we can heal our past if we wish?

Suppose we can see what we imagined was a difficult experience or trauma in our childhood in a new way? For example, I realize now with hindsight that what I thought was a lonely, desolate, wasted period of my life was actually a time of considerable blessing. It opened a door to a new experience of myself. It helped instil a longing for deeper meaning and happiness in life.

I felt alone and abandoned for four long years, from the age of eight to the age of 12, when I was evacuated from London to the Devon countryside in the early days of the Blitz. It's true that my aunt Eva was there to take care of me. But the cottage where we lived was quite remote, and I sure felt alone. I had no friends. And with Dad away as a war correspondent in India and Burma, and Mom working in Harrods bookshop in London, I was separated from both of them in what seemed a strange, alien environment.

Before I was evacuated, I'd lived with my mother on the fifth floor of an apartment block in central London. What did I know of the countryside? I was a child of the city. But here's what I see now that I didn't see before.

Being sent to live in a remote cottage at the end of a quiet Devonshire lane — a cottage with no electricity, of course — gave me the opportunity to suddenly become aware of two things that have proved to be critical components of my life ever since.

It opened my eyes to the magic of Nature. And it introduced me to stillness, the primeval stillness that we are conditioned to fear but which I now know is the source of all true wisdom, and the door to true meaning and happiness no matter what our age.

What I thought of as wasted years opened my eyes to the magic of birds, fields, and books. I experienced the simple happiness of reading, picking blackberries, and exploring Devon lanes. I was given the gift of safety. I see how miraculous it was when my Mom came down to visit from London and we climbed on our bikes and went for long bike rides together to favorite spots on the North Devon coast.

I remember how blissful it was to snuggle in my feather bed while my mother, in one of her visits, read to me from Dickens. And I remember the peaceful evenings with my Aunt Eva and cousin Joan — after Aunt had lit the Aladdin lamp — eating apples we had picked earlier from the little orchard at the rear of the cottage. I am thankful for all of it.

How about your early years? Is there anything you would like to heal, bless, and make whole as you bring it to the light of now, the light of your present day awareness?

As we touch the timelessness of our own unconquerable spirit is anything beyond the reach of our love?

CHAPTER 24

Are There Surprising Benefits in Challenging Times?

> *"Our greatest weakness lies in giving up. The most certain way to succeed is always to try just one more time."*
> – Thomas Edison

We can think of past traumas in our lives as afflictions, which perhaps they were, in a way. But there is another way to look at difficult times.

The lessons you and I have learned and the ways in which we navigated our way back from hell may assist others and be of interest to others as they face similar challenges in their own life.

More and more people are flexing their entrepreneurial muscles and creating interesting, inspiring products based in their own unique experiences. The products make a big difference in other people's lives at the same time they create a living.

This is what Martha Beck, the celebrated life coach says in her great new book, *Finding Your Way in a Wild New World*: "A lot of people tell me, 'I need to find my passion.' They rarely realize that the word 'passion' is from the Latin *pati*, 'to suffer", or that passion originally meant 'pain' (as in The Passion of the Christ)...

"Wayfinders of all cultures know that healing the self from any kind of torment is the groundwork for healing others, for creating positive change in the world of Form and thereby establishing your career, your life's work." It's a win-win idea, she affirms.

Martha goes on to say: "Without deep suffering, menders can't possibly help the people who will later look into their eyes and ask, "Can I really be happy after living through this hell?"

Count on it, she says. "Whatever you're suffering is leading you toward your life's purpose. It's giving you depth, resonance, street cred. It's turning you into a healer – on one condition: you must not stop tracking."

CHAPTER 25

7 Gifts of a Loving Universe

> *"Love never fails."*
> – 1 Corinthians 13.8

We are not as weak or alone as we may think. The universe has given us 7 gifts to help us flourish and realize our dreams:

1. Patience makes it possible to not only bear anguish and trauma but follow our dream and discover who we truly are.
2. Gratitude opens the door to wisdom. It makes it possible for us to change, and to grow. If we have believed a lie, or our attitude to someone is wrong – we can change. Gratitude opens a door to greater meaning and wholeness.

3. Courage is the creative power that makes it possible for us to meet the challenges of our lives and give the unique gift we came into the world to give.

4. Compassion sees the pain of the world, but it also sees the beauty and oneness of creation.

5. The world tries to convince us that happiness is outside ourselves but it is given to us at birth and all you have to do is reclaim what is already yours.

6. Freedom. Nothing needs to change for us to be free. We can be free right now regardless of our circumstances as we remember our own timeless, unspoilt presence.

7. Love. You are loved. The universe sees you, admires you, and loves you, because you are part of It.

The universe would not exist if we did not exist. The older I get, the more I realize that the universe is kinder, wiser, and infinitely more loving than our mind will ever realize. But while we will never understand this miraculous universe mentally, we can experience it. We can learn to love it, admire it, and see it as an accurate reflection of our own true nature.

CHAPTER 26

The Power of Patience

> *"You can learn many things from children. How much patience you have, for instance."*
> – Franklin P. Jones

The power of patience is all too easily overlooked in our fast paced culture. But it's absolutely critical to lasting happiness and inner peace.

True, with more and more people demanding immediate gratification it might seem patience has become obsolete.

But whatever your age, and whatever your life situation, nurturing this calm and noble quality will yield the same rich rewards today that it always has throughout the entire run of human history.

Of course, it goes without saying that patience can never really be isolated from any of the other qualities of our own true character. "Patience is the companion of wisdom," said St. Augustine, and he was absolutely right. Patience needs the balance of wisdom – and it needs the balance of courage too.

Here are 5 reasons why the power of patience is so important in your life.

1. Patience helps us fulfill our dreams.

   If you are short of patience, even though your dream may be an admirable one, you will simply not have the strength and persistence necessary to sustain you through the inevitable disappointments and setbacks that life brings.

2. You need patience to become whole.

   What was true in ages past is still true today. "Let patience have her perfect works, that ye may be perfect and entire, wanting nothing."

3. Patience is required to fully forgive.

   Often, we may think we have forgiven someone – perhaps God himself – for some past injustice, but then the pain and resentment rise up in us again. Do we give up, and allow negative emotions to fester freely in us until we die?

Or do we summon the Angel of patience to our aid and forgive at a deeper level?

4. Patience helps us see others in a true light.

   It takes time and perseverance to see through our first impressions — which may or may not be all that accurate – and come to know the real person behind the outer mask.

5. The power of patience nourishes all other human virtues.

   As St. Augustine suggested, if we want to develop wisdom, we will need the help of its companion, patience. Or how about compassion? Perhaps some people are born with naturally compassionate natures — but it's my guess that even compassion needs the nourishment of patience at times.

CHAPTER 27

Closing Thoughts

> *"Though we march to the music of our time, our mission is timeless."*
> – President Bill Clinton

Two qualities essential to a happy life are being able to forgive ourselves – how can we forgive others if we can't forgive ourselves? – and being willing to take personal responsibility for our choices and actions.

They are aspects of our true character but it takes all the courage and humility that is in us, in my experience, to be true to these qualities. It's worth it though. It really is. What did Shakespeare say? "This above all, to thine own self be true, for it must follow as night follows day that thou canst not then be false to any man."

Another aspect of being true to ourselves is having the courage to go against the beliefs of others – or even "mainstream" opinions – if it conflicts with our own sense of destiny or our own sense of what is true or not true. It was sad, tragic in a way, but like many, I had no choice but to distance myself from my family when I was young. My parents simply could not understand my passionate desire to find the truth of life. It seemed too remote and apparently insubstantial.

It takes radical self-reliance to be true to ourselves, so that we refuse, for example, to believe the widely-held belief that as we age, we become irrelevant. Or that we are somehow inherently flawed and imperfect.

It takes radical self-reliance to face our fears and open our heart to a new vision of reality that acknowledges our true nature as spiritual beings who have come into this world with a unique gift to give.

I wish for you what I wish for myself, that together we may uncover more and more of the masterpiece we truly are.

You are beautiful. You are perfect. You are an expression of Eternal Love. Nothing can enhance your true nature and nothing can diminish it and it doesn't need more schooling, thank you. All it needs is to be given expression through us as clearly and consistently as we know how and the entire planet rejoices.

I send you love and best wishes. I'd love to hear from you anytime via my blog or at the email address at the end of my biography.

THE END

About Christopher Foster

I started blogging in May 2009 and have been called "the world's oldest, newest blogger." I'm the author of five books including *The Raven Who Spoke with God*, a fable that shows how if we trust life and listen to the nudges of our own heart, we will find the fulfillment we desire. First published on 9/11, the book has been translated into 11 languages and is available now in Kindle format at Amazon.

My raven book is my favorite. I wrote it soon after moving to Denver from British Columbia to marry JoAnn 15 years ago. It was a huge step for both of us. JoAnn noticed I liked to go to a nearby coffee shop in the afternoon, and one day she said, "You're in the coffee shop anyway, why don't you write a book while you're there?" So that's what I did. She's a wise lady.

I was born in London in 1932. I was an only child and lived a normal British middle class life (if you don't count WWII) until I was 16, when things began to get wild. I told my parents at lunch one day that what I wanted most in life was to find the truth. It didn't go over well. Dad and I got into a fierce argument which ended suddenly when he lost his temper and slapped me hard across the side of my head.

Dad was a reporter all his life, and I started out the same way, working on newspapers and magazines in London, Southern Rhodesia (now Zimbabwe), New Zealand, and Canada. The longing to find a deeper meaning in existence took me finally to British Columbia, where I hitch-hiked to Alaska, got a job on a ranch, and then worked as a reporter on the Daily Colonist in Victoria.

Through one of life's synchronicities I met a British nobleman who became my mentor and changed my life. He was Lord Martin Cecil – a descendant of Lord Burghley, chief adviser to Queen Elizabeth I – who as a young man, had given up his British aristocratic heritage to come out to the wilds of British Columbia and manage his father's cattle ranch.

I loved Lord Martin and became part of a spiritual community he had founded in 1946 in 100 Mile House, BC. I was a member of the community for 36 years and thought it would be my home forever. But after my mentor died suddenly in 1988 the community went into decline. A few years later, at the age of 63, I had no choice but to return to the world I had abandoned in the idealism of my youth.

I was in despair. It was like stepping off a precipice. But I know now it was a blessing in disguise. It opened a door to a new life and made it possible for me to find a growing sense of true freedom and purpose.

I've loved writing all my life. I wrote my first story in an old scrapbook at the age of 7 with bombs falling all around the apartment in central London where my Mum and I lived in the early days of the Blitz. Dad was away in the army as a war correspondent, first of all in Dover, covering the Battle of Britain, and later in India and Burma. He took part in a number of landings with the British Army against the Japanese – armed with a typewriter instead of a gun.

Today, as I enter my 80s, I'm armed with a computer which makes it possible for me to embark upon wild adventures such as blogging and writing digital books.

I'm happier than I have ever been in my life. There are challenges, of course. But I am so thankful for the goodness of life and the wisdom that calls to each of us in these troubled times and the opportunity we have to give the gift that is ours to give. With love and blessings to you.

For more from Christopher, please visit my blog at www.thehappyseeker.com *or write me at* christopherjfoster@comcast.net.

The Raven Who Spoke with God

A Fable for Our Troubled Times

> *"It soars. This is no ordinary book, and no ordinary bird."*
> – Sunday Oklahoman.

> *"In his latest work, Christopher Foster explores such themes as death and grieving, learning to be safe with an open heart, the meaning of home, the power of stillness, the function of Being, and the oneness of human and animal life. As I read the book, I thought, what a wonderful way to introduce people of all ages to these timeless themes. Its easy style and simplicity of expression make it a perfect vehicle for deep conversation and insightful learning."*
> – Communaissance Magazine

The Raven Who Spoke with God is an inspiring story anyone can relate to in these uncertain times.

Are you facing challenges? Do you feel as if your life is off track in some way? Do you have a nagging sense something is missing in your life, or your dream is slipping away?

Joshua is a brave, sensitive young raven with an excruciating decision to make. Will he follow his dream to restore the true honor of the raven as a messenger and guardian of humanity? Or will he allow the scorn and disapproval of his father and siblings to influence him so that he settles for a normal, "comfortable" raven life like his brethren?

Alone, scared and hungry, he gives up everything that is familiar and embarks on a journey into the unknown – "The Hero's Journey," as it has been called – in which he learns important life lessons vital to us all.

- Trust your own unconquerable spirit.
- Listen to the wisdom of your own heart.
- Discover new friends and mentors who will help you fulfill your dream.

Please go here for more information about The Raven Who Spoke with God, *on sale at Amazon in Kindle format, with more versions to come:*

http://www.amazon.com/dp/B007OLLQYM

www.ingramcontent.com/pod-product-compliance
Lightning Source LLC
LaVergne TN
LVHW020638100826
845148LV00012B/2237

* 9 7 8 0 9 7 1 1 7 9 6 1 5 *